Maya, Incas, and Aztec

Follow the timeline across these pages to trace the rise and fall of the Maya, Incas, and Aztecs.

Aztec valley
People move into the Valley of Mexico. They will later start the Aztec Empire.

Modern statue of the Inca ruler Pachacuti

Pachacuti
An Inca ruler, Pachacuti, leads armies to defeat rivals and make an empire in Peru.

Moctezuma II watching a comet

Moctezuma II
The last Aztec leader, Moctezuma II, is crowned.

Alvarado
Spanish invader Alvarado and his soldiers defeat the Maya in Guatemala.

1200 CE	1325 CE	1438 CE	1471 CE	1502 CE	1519–1521 CE	1524 CE	1531–1532 CE

Model of Aztec god Xipe Totec

Yupanqui
Pachacuti's son, Topa Inca Yupanqui (ruled 1471–1493), doubles the size of the Inca Empire.

Pizarro
Francisco Pizarro takes over the Inca Empire for the Spanish.

Aztec empire
The Aztecs begin building their first city, Tenochtitlan.

Cortés
Hernando Cortés and his small army of Spanish soldiers conquer the Aztecs in two years.

Things to find out:

DK findout!

Maya,
Incas, and Aztecs

Author: Brian Williams
Historical consultant: Dr Caroline Dodds Pennock

DK | Penguin Random House

Editors Anwesha Dutta, Kathleen Teece
Senior art editor Ann Cannings
Senior editor Marie Greenwood
Project editor Ishani Nandi
Art editor Jaileen Kaur
Assistant editor Shalini Agrawal
Managing editors Laura Gilbert,
Alka Thakur Hazarika
Managing art editors Diane Peyton Jones,
Romi Chakraborty
Jacket designer Suzena Sengupta
Jacket coordinator Francesca Young
DTP designers Jagtar Singh, Dheeraj Singh
Picture researcher Sumita Khatwani
CTS manager Balwant Singh
Pre-production producer Tony Phipps
Senior producer Isabell Schart
Art director Martin Wilson
Publishing director Sarah Larter
Educational consultant Jacqueline Harris

First published in Great Britain in 2018 by
Dorling Kindersley Limited
DK, One Embassy Gardens, 8 Viaduct Gardens,
London, SW11 7BW

The authorised representative in the EEA is
Dorling Kindersley Verlag GmbH. Arnulfstr. 124,
80636 Munich, Germany

A CIP catalogue record for this book
is available from the British Library.
ISBN: 978-0-2413-1868-3

Printed in China

For the curious
www.dk.com

MIX
Paper from
responsible sources
FSC™ C018179

This book was made with Forest
Stewardship Council™ certified
paper – one small step in DK's
commitment to a sustainable future.
For more information go to
www.dk.com/our-green-pledge

Contents

Macaw, kept
as pets by
the Incas

Maya pyramid

BCE/CE
When you see the letters BCE, it means
Before the Common Era, which began
in the year 1CE (Common Era).

How to say it
Learn how to say words and the names
of gods and places from the Maya,
Inca, and Aztec civilizations using the
guide at the back of this book.

Rabbit's foot fern, used by the Aztecs for healing

Passion flower, used in Aztec medicine

Inca ruler

Gold llama

Quechua dolls

Three civilizations

The Maya, Incas, and Aztecs were great civilizations of the American continents. A civilization is a society that shares the same way of life. You can still visit the remains of their cities today, deep in jungles and high on mountains.

Aztecs

The Aztecs were powerful people who lived in Mexico from around 1300–1500s CE. The Aztecs believed that gods controlled the world. They sacrificed humans to feed the gods, giving them energy.

Sun stone showing the Aztec Sun god, Tonatiuh, in the centre

North America

Central Americ

These three civilizations stretched from southern North America to South America.

KEY

Aztecs

Maya

Incas

Maya

The Maya people are still around today. They have lived in Central America since around 2000BCE. They built jungle cities and created early systems of maths, science, and writing.

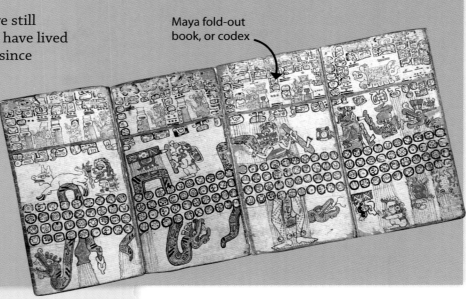

Maya fold-out book, or codex

South America

Incas

The Incas had an empire in South America. This means they ruled neighbouring lands. The empire began in around 1200CE and lasted until the early 1500s CE. They built cities in the Andes mountains in Peru.

The Incas mined gold to make objects such as this figure, which was left inside a tomb.

Maya

We've stepped back in time to Yucatán, Mexico, in 1500CE. This is the land of the star-gazing, pyramid-building Maya. Let's ask a couple of them about Maya life, which stretches all the way back to around 2000BCE.

Q: Is there a king of the Maya?

A: No, the Maya civilization is divided into cities, and each city has its own king. Sometimes the kings battle with each other.

Q: Can you tell us about your pyramids?

A: We hand-cut stones into blocks and slot them together. We build temples on top of the pyramids for our gods.

Q: Why do you worship gods?

A: Our gods control what goes on in the world, such as the weather. If they are upset, they might make bad things happen.

Q: How do you keep the gods happy?

A: We have festivals and make human sacrifices to different gods. To bring rain, we make sacrifices to the rain god.

! REALLY?

After a **battle** between Maya cities, the winning king might **sacrifice** the losing king.

A: We record the days and times of battles, kings' deaths, and other events. We write the information on paper, and carve it on stone columns.

Q: How do you keep track of your history?

A: Our writing system is made up of glyphs, which are small pictures representing words.

Q: Can you tell us more about your writing?

A: We are wearing huge headdresses. We often make them look like animals or birds.

Q: What are you wearing on your heads?

Incas

We've time-travelled all the way back to the Inca Empire, South America, in 1500CE. At this time, the Incas have been around for about 300 years. Let's ask a couple of Incas about their world of gods, mountain-top cities, and llamas.

Q. What is an empire and how big is yours?

A: An empire is a group of lands ruled by the same leader. Our people have conquered many lands in western South America.

Q. Who is your leader?

A: Our leader is the Sapa Inca. He is sacred and has many wives, including the Mama Coya. Her son will be the next Sapa Inca.

Q. How do you build mountain-top cities?

A: We cut stone into blocks and fit them together. All ordinary Incas have to spend some time helping to build Inca roads or cities.

A: This is a spindle whorl for spinning llama fur into wool.

Q. What's that you're holding?

Q. What will happen when your leader dies?

A: His body will be made into a mummy, or preserved. The mummy will be kept in a special store, and brought out for ceremonies.

Q. Can you tell us what you're holding?

A: This set of strings is a *quipu*. It has knots to record numbers and other information.

Q. What is your most important animal?

A: We have millions of llamas for meat, milk, and wool. Llamas can also carry packs on their backs up hills.

Q. Do you mix with people from other lands?

A: We trade, or swap, goods such as cloth with other people. Some of our neighbours hate us and we sometimes go to war with them.

Aztecs

The final stop in our time-travelling adventure is the Aztec Empire, in Mexico. The year is 1518CE. The Aztecs had started out, in the 1000s CE, as a people who wandered from place to place. But they now live in bustling, built-up cities. Let's ask a warrior and a teacher about their lives.

Q: What is the Aztec Empire?

A: An empire is made up of multiple lands with the same ruler. Our ruler lives in the city of Tenochtitlan.

Q: Who is the Aztec leader?

A: Our current leader is the mighty emperor Moctezuma II. No ordinary person dares look at his face.

Q: What's it like being an Aztec warrior?

A: We fear no one in battle, and we have good weapons. If we capture enemies, we sacrifice them to the gods.

Q: Do you follow a religion?

A: We believe in many gods, who control the world. Priests keep the gods happy through human sacrifice.

Q: What kind of jobs do your people do?

A: Warriors and priests do important jobs. Local leaders run schools, food stores, and temples. Many women run their homes.

Q: How do you record Aztec history?

A: We tell stories and write them down in books. We also paint pictures and carve images in stone.

Q: Are your books like ours?

A: Not really. Our type of book is called a codex, with pages folded like a fan. We make paper from bark, and every page is handwritten.

Society

The Maya, Incas, and Aztecs were all well-organized societies, divided into different levels, or classes. While the Incas and Aztecs each had an emperor at the head, Maya society was divided into cities with their own rulers, and had no single leader.

Sapa Inca

Inca society
Inca society was shaped like a pyramid. There was the emperor and family at the top. Then came the priests and nobles. Most people were at the bottom.

Wives
The emperor had many wives and children. Wives were chosen from noble families.

High priest
The high priest, or Willac Umu, was a nobleman, and was often related to the emperor.

Willac Umu

Clan groups
Other relatives of the Sapa Inca were called *panacas*. They wore gold plugs in their ears as a mark of bravery in battle.

Panacas

Farmers

Emperor

The emperor was called the Sapa Inca, or great Inca. He had supreme power over land and people. The Incas believed he was a descendant of the Sun god, Inti.

Aztec men and women

Men ruled in Aztec society, but women had rights, too. A woman could inherit property after her husband died, and ask for a divorce if her marriage was unhappy. Both boys and girls went to school.

A page from a codex (book) showing Aztec parents teaching skills to their children

Chief wife

The Sapa Inca's chief wife was often his sister. She was called the Mama Coya. Only one of her sons could be the next Sapa Inca.

Priests

Men and women could be priests. The women that were chosen were called *mamakuna*. They were picked as children, and trained as temple priestesses.

Mamakuna

Lords

Local lords, or *curacas*, helped run the empire, along with officials such as accountants and tax collectors.

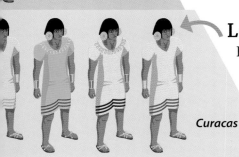

Curacas

! WOW!

One piece of Inca **royal clothing** was made out of **bat hair.**

Ordinary people

Ordinary people included craftspeople, farmers, soldiers, and servants. Slaves, usually prisoners of war, were right at the bottom.

Soldiers

Servants

Home

Most people lived in small, simple houses, either in cities or villages. While most Maya and Aztec houses had walls made from dried mud, Inca houses were made from stone.

Aztec and Maya
Forests provided wood for houses. A roof of palm leaves and branches kept out rain and sun.

Inca
Family groups lived together in stone houses. They had small windows to keep out rain and wind.

Daily life

For most people, whether Maya, Aztec, or Inca, daily life meant hard work and obeying the rules. Everyone knew their duties and their place in society – men and women, rich and poor, young and old. If the gods were kind, familes had a home, clothes, and enough food to live on.

! WOW!

Inca houses were specially built so that they did not collapse in earthquakes.

Work

Every day, people worked out in the fields to grow food. Men and women shared the work. People wore simple, tunic-style work clothes. Only nobles wore fine robes.

Field work
This picture shows Inca farmers harvesting the corn crop.

Families

Children were welcome "gifts from the gods". Men were at the head of most families. But when men went to war, women ran the home and family business.

Family scene
This picture is from a 1500s CE codex (book) about Aztec life.

Slavery

The Aztecs and Maya owned slaves. Many Aztec slaves were captured during wars. Some very poor Aztecs chose to become slaves, and others were made slaves as punishment. Generally, slaves were not treated badly. Aztec slaves could marry. They could also buy their freedom and even own other slaves.

Aztec slaves

Farming

The Maya, Aztec, and Inca peoples were expert farmers. They tended crops on farmland ranging from warm, wet lowlands to cold, dry highlands. They farmed in the middle of lakes and on steep mountain slopes. All three civilizations grew a wide variety of plants for food, but the most important was maize.

This Inca carving was used in rituals. It was a digging stick like those used to dig fields for farming. It was also a water jug.

Farming by hand

Maya, Inca, and Aztec farmers had no machines and no horses or oxen to help them. Workers dug the land with wooden sticks. They also used foot-ploughs – these were pointed poles with foot rests. Cutting tools were made from stone or copper.

Maya

With about 10 million people to feed, Maya farmers had to work hard. Villagers got together and worked in teams. Nobles acted as farm managers. Because they lived in a warm climate, the Maya could grow all sorts of food, including hot and spicy chili peppers. This meant that their food was full of flavour.

Avocado

Aztecs

The Aztecs, too, lived in a warm land. Here, beans, pumpkin, tomatoes, and maize all grew well. They ate maize in lots of different ways, including as a paste. They also made it into a drink. They picked cacao beans to make their nobles' favourite drink: chocolate.

Beans

Maize

Incas

Inca men and women worked hard in teams in the Andes mountains. They often sang as they planted potatoes, a grain called quinoa, and other crops that could survive the harsh weather. Higher up in the mountains, they herded llamas and alpacas. Lower down, farmers grew squash, fruit, and nuts.

Quino

Sweet potato

Chili peppers

Canals

The Maya dug ditches and built canals to carry water to their fields. This farming method is called irrigation, and the Maya people were skilled at it. By making sure their crops were well watered, Maya farmers could grow enough crops to feed all their people.

Pumpkin

Tomatoes

Floating fields

The Aztecs used Lake Texcoco and marshland as extra farms. They made "floating fields" called *chinampas*. Male and female farmers planted these muddy islands with crops. The *chinampas* were kept rich and fertile with animal dung, brought by canoe from the city.

Potatoes

Terraces

To make extra farmland, the Incas built terraced fields. They had stone walls that absorbed the Sun's heat by day, and so helped to keep plants warm at night. Farmers planted in layers in the earth: first maize, then beans that would grow up the maize stalks, with squash at the bottom.

Food

The Maya, Incas, and Aztecs ate some foods that you'll recognise, and some you probably won't! Growing food was a daily job for most people. They also kept animals, hunted, or went to a market to get meat and fish.

Maguey worms

Insects
Crunchy grasshoppers were roasted or added to soups and stews by the Maya and the Aztecs. Caterpillars called maguey worms were also used in Maya and Aztec cooking, or as quick snacks.

Grasshopper

Algae

Vanilla

Flavourings
The Maya, Incas, and Aztecs used chili peppers to make spicy food. The Aztecs added algae, which grows on top of water, to bread. The Aztecs and Maya loved sweet vanilla.

Chili powder

Quinoa

Grains
The Incas cooked quinoa seeds in porridge and stews. They also ground the seeds into flour to make bread. The Aztecs made similar dishes and breads with amaranth seeds.

Amaranth

Opossum

Armadillo

Meat
People caught fish and hunted birds and deer. The Incas lived off llamas and guinea pigs. More unusual meat included iguanas and opossums, which both the Aztecs and Maya enjoyed. The Aztecs even ate armadillos!

Iguana

Llama

Prickly pear
cactus fruit

Tomatoes

Fruits

The Aztec and Maya ate lots of healthy fruits, which were picked in the wild or grown at home. The forests provided many kinds of juicy fruits, such as wild tomatoes. These were small and yellow.

Pineapple

Papaya

Avocados

Squash

Mushrooms

Vegetables

The Maya, Incas, and Aztecs all ate maize. It was eaten from the cob, or ground into flour to make tortilla bread. The Incas ate lots of potatoes, while both the Maya and Aztecs cooked squash, and all three ate mushrooms.

Maize cob

Potatoes

Chocolate

The Maya and Aztecs were the first people to turn beans from the cacao tree into drinking chocolate. Here's how they made a delicious chocolate drink!

1 Preparing the beans
Cacao beans were picked and dried in the hot sun.

2 Grinding up
The shells were peeled off and the beans were crushed into an oily powder.

3 Mixing
The powder was mixed with water. The mixture was stirred to make a foamy paste.

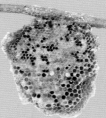

4 Spices and flavours
Spices were added for flavour, or honey to sweeten, and the drink was then ready!

Honeycomb

Chilies

Children

It was tough being a Maya, Inca, or Aztec child. From toddler-age, boys were taught their father's work, such as fishing, and girls learnt household skills, such as weaving. Bad behaviour was punished by parents, but families were still loving to each other.

Aztec girl with a broom

Grain-grinding stone

Aztec
A tiny model broom was given to baby girls as a sign of their future work – to clean the house. Girls would also do other housework, such as cooking. They were trained to do jobs such as teaching, and a few learned how to be priestesses. Children often learned their parents' jobs, such as farming. All boys trained to be warriors at military school.

Fathers taught sons how to hunt, farm, and catch fish.

Aztec father and son fishing with nets

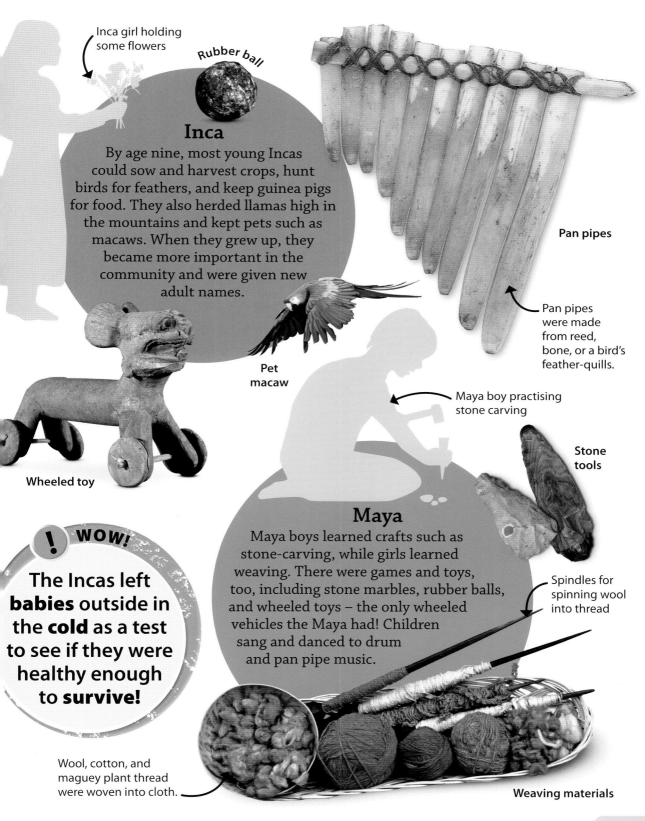

Inca girl holding some flowers

Rubber ball

Inca

By age nine, most young Incas could sow and harvest crops, hunt birds for feathers, and keep guinea pigs for food. They also herded llamas high in the mountains and kept pets such as macaws. When they grew up, they became more important in the community and were given new adult names.

Pan pipes

Pan pipes were made from reed, bone, or a bird's feather-quills.

Pet macaw

Wheeled toy

Maya boy practising stone carving

Stone tools

Maya

Maya boys learned crafts such as stone-carving, while girls learned weaving. There were games and toys, too, including stone marbles, rubber balls, and wheeled toys – the only wheeled vehicles the Maya had! Children sang and danced to drum and pan pipe music.

Spindles for spinning wool into thread

! WOW!

The Incas left **babies** outside in the **cold** as a test to see if they were healthy enough to **survive!**

Wool, cotton, and maguey plant thread were woven into cloth.

Weaving materials

Tenochtitlan

The Aztec capital, Tenochtitlan, was home to around 200,000 people. Built on an island in Lake Texcoco, this "floating city" had streets, canals, royal palaces, and a busy market. On top of high temples, priests made sacrifices to the gods.

AROUND THE SITE

A   **Sacred centre** At the heart of the city were pyramid-shaped temples, and palaces for the emperor and his relatives.

B   **Market** People came here to trade goods such as food, feathers, animal skins, cloth, pottery, and gold.

C   **Canals** The Aztecs built canals from the centre of the city to the outskirts. They were used to transport people and goods.

D   **Canoes** People paddled dugout canoes, made by hollowing out trees. Some canoes were 15 m (50 ft) long.

E   **Sacrificial altar** Priests performed human sacrifices on the altar in honour of the gods.

F   **Temple steps** A flight of steep steps led to the sacrificial altar at the top of the temple.

G   **Great Temple** At 60 m (196 ft) high, this was the biggest of the city's temples. It was also one of the last, finished in 1487CE.

Rain god's shrine
This part of the temple
was dedicated to the
god of rain, Tlaloc.

Sun god's shrine
This shrine was built
for Huitzilopochtli
– the supreme
Aztec god.

ouses
ost city homes
ere single-storey,
ud-brick houses,
ith thatched roofs.

E

F

G

Ritual sacrifice
People gathered and
watched as human
sacrifices were made
to the gods.

Machu Picchu

This magnificent Inca site nestles high up in the Andes mountains in Peru. Built in the 1400s CE, it may have been used as a royal estate and a sacred religious place for Inca leaders. Today, visitors come to wonder at Machu Picchu's 200 buildings linked by 3,000 stone steps.

Hiram Bingham and his mule

Hiram Bingham
In 1911, US explorer Hiram Bingham trekked high into the Andes. He was searching for the lost city of the Incas, called Vilcabamba. He was led to Machu Picchu by local people.

①

②

③

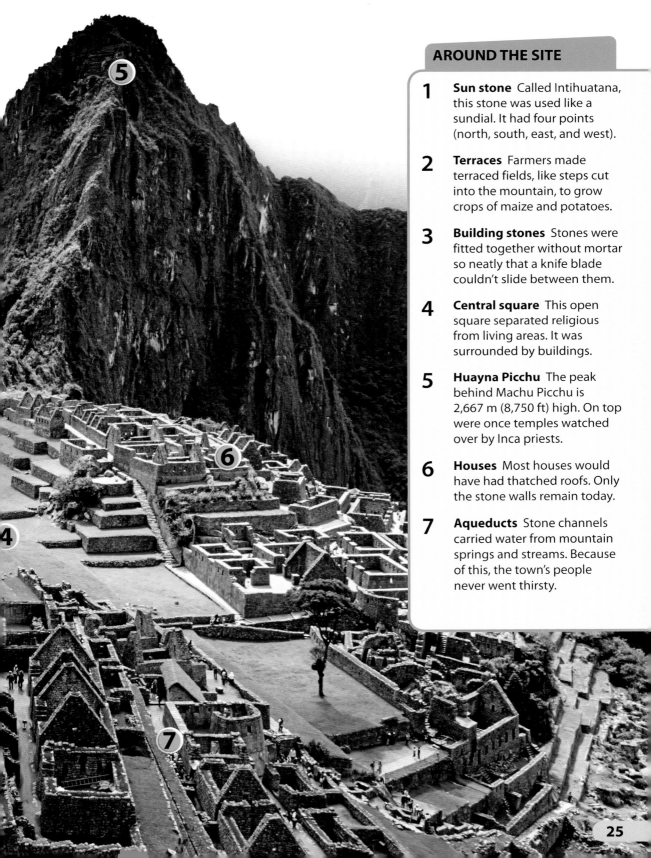

AROUND THE SITE

1 **Sun stone** Called Intihuatana, this stone was used like a sundial. It had four points (north, south, east, and west).

2 **Terraces** Farmers made terraced fields, like steps cut into the mountain, to grow crops of maize and potatoes.

3 **Building stones** Stones were fitted together without mortar so neatly that a knife blade couldn't slide between them.

4 **Central square** This open square separated religious from living areas. It was surrounded by buildings.

5 **Huayna Picchu** The peak behind Machu Picchu is 2,667 m (8,750 ft) high. On top were once temples watched over by Inca priests.

6 **Houses** Most houses would have had thatched roofs. Only the stone walls remain today.

7 **Aqueducts** Stone channels carried water from mountain springs and streams. Because of this, the town's people never went thirsty.

Gods

People believed gods controlled all life on Earth, from the weather to wars. They worshipped gods in temples and offered sacrifices to keep the gods happy. Each civilization had their own gods, but some gods were shared.

Viracocha

This stick-carrying man was the Inca creator-god. He made the Earth, Sun, Moon, people, and other gods. He left everyday matters such as the weather to gods of less importance.

Ixchel

This old woman with a headdress in the shape of a snake was the Maya goddess of midwives, medicine, and the Moon. She is often shown with a jug of water, which she could pour as rain.

Quetzalcoatl

He was a chief Aztec god, but the Maya also worshipped him under the name Kukulkan. He controlled the wind and was in charge of priests, learning, and death. He could take the form of a man, or a huge serpent with feathers.

Huitzilopochtli

This Aztec god was in charge of war and the Sun. He was also said to have guided the Aztecs to their first city, Tenochtitlan. He was quick and fierce, and he could appear as an eagle.

Tlaloc

Tlaloc was the Aztec god of rain and water. He made crops grow, but could also bring droughts. He was painted with goggle-like eyes. The Maya had a similar god, named Chac.

Inca mythology

Like many peoples, the Incas told stories, or myths, about their gods and how the world was made. Every Inca child was told the story of how two Inca heroes, Manco Capac and Mama Ocllo, founded the Inca Empire.

Viracocha

At the start of time, the supreme being, Viracocha, created the world. He put three chief gods in charge of Earth: Inti, the god of the Sun; Illapu, the god of rain and thunder; and Mama Quilla, the goddess of the Moon.

The first people behaved badly. This made the gods angry, and so they sent a great flood. Water covered the Earth.

Families escaped up mountains with their llama flocks. Many other wild animals managed to get away, too.

However, over time, people started to misbehave again. The land became wild and dangerous. Manco Capac, son of Inti, and his sister-wife Mama Ocllo set out to find a better place to live.

Success!

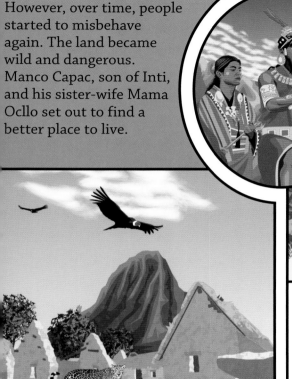

Inti gave Manco Capac and Mama Ocllo a gold stick for the journey. After a long trek, they reached a valley. Manco tested the ground with the stick, and it vanished into the soil. This was the sign that they had found the fertile Cusco Valley.

Manco and Mama Ocllo settled in the valley. They taught people how to live a civilized life. People learnt how to herd llamas, grow maize, dig canals, and make pottery. Mama Ocllo showed women how to sew, spin wool, and weave cloth.

They built a great city, Cusco. It had a mighty stone fortress, Sacsayhuaman, and a temple to Inti the Sun god. And so that was how the Inca Empire began, with Manco Capac its first emperor.

Ceremonies

For the Maya, Aztecs, and Incas, ceremonies were important events in the yearly calendar. Religious festivals took place when crops were planted and harvested. Emperors and priests made sacrifices to gods. There were celebrations held in honour of new babies, young people, and dead ancestors.

Inca nobles digging with foot ploughs before planting

Sun-worship

The Sun was especially important to the Incas. They believed their emperor was the Sun god's son. Incas celebrated the Sun's journey across the sky with ceremonies in December and June.

An Inca warrior offering drink to the Sun god

Planting ceremony

In spring, Inca nobles dug the first furrows in the ground for sowing seeds. The people then planted crops. At harvest time, everyone gathered for a thanksgiving ceremony. This lasted for eight days.

Sacrifices

The Maya and Aztecs offered their gods human sacrifices. Victims were thrown into sacred wells or killed in temple ceremonies. The Incas and Aztecs made sacrifices on mountain peaks.

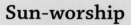

! WOW!

The Incas believed objects called huaca, such as certain rocks or stone figures, had sacred powers.

Aztec stone knife used in sacrifices

Ear-piercing ritual

At about 14, a noble Inca boy had his ears pierced and discs inserted. This showed he was now a man. The boy climbed a sacred peak, and promised to fight for his Sun emperor. His family gave him a cloak. This was a sign that he was now a warrior.

Inca ceremonial mask, showing ear discs

Flower wars

Aztecs often took part in "flower wars", sometimes after crop failure. Here, warriors fought not to kill, but to take captives. The prisoners were sacrificed to the gods in the hope of a better harvest.

Incas offering drink to the mummy of a dead leader

Mummy ceremony

The Incas preserved their dead emperors as mummies. Each November, the ruling Inca offered royal mummies food and drink, so that his ancestors would help him.

Aztec jaguar warrior (right) about to sacrifice a captured warrior

War

War was part of life. The Maya and Incas sent armies into battle, but the Aztecs were especially feared warriors. Battles began with armies far apart, shooting arrows and javelins from complex machines. Closer fighting with clubs and knives came next. Prisoners were taken for human sacrifice.

Knives

Razor-sharp knives were made from a volcanic stone called obsidian. Aztecs cut their enemies' legs to make them fall.

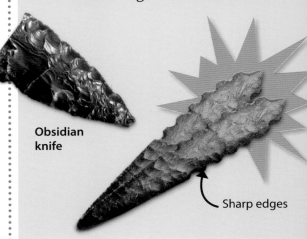

Obsidian knife

Sharp edges

Sharp obsidian blades inserted into a wooden club

Club

An Aztec warrior would swing a wooden club called a *maquahuitl* like a sword. About 1 m (39 in) long, it was so sharp it could slice off an enemy's head.

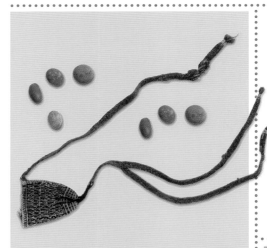

SLING

The sling could fling a stone over 200 m (650 ft). It was made from strong plant-fibre, and was whirled around to release the stone. Slingers chose stones with care before a battle.

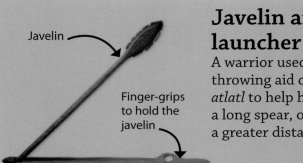

Javelin

Finger-grips to hold the javelin

Javelin and launcher

A warrior used a throwing aid called an *atlatl* to help him throw a long spear, or javelin, a greater distance.

An Aztec ruler is said to have worn this headdress.

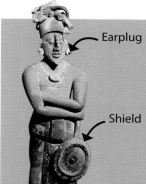

Maya warrior

Earplug

Shield

This clay warrior has earplugs, a headdress, and a shield. A Maya warrior had a tuft of hair on his head that he switched from the left to the right after taking his first prisoner.

IEADDRESS

ther headdresses made
h-ranking Aztec warriors
k taller and fiercer.
e one above is made
n about 500 feathers
n the quetzal bird.
Aztec fighters wore
-body jaguar or
le costumes.

Feather headdress

SHIELD

Shields were made from animal skin or wood. Some were brightly decorated, and were meant to scare the enemy as well as to protect warriors' bodies. Warriors also wore padded cotton body-armour.

Aztecs stuck feathers on their shields.

Axe

A stone axe, similar to tools used by farmers to break up hard soil, made a useful weapon. Most axes had stone heads, but some had sharper heads of copper metal.

Stone axe

Metal head

Bow and arrow

Archers with bows stood in the front of the battle line, with slingers and javelin-throwers. Their bows were 1.5 m (5 ft) long, and could shoot arrows up to 100 m (330 ft).

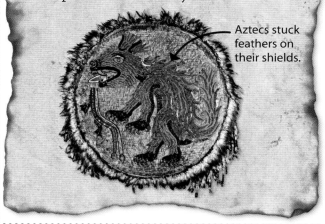

Arrow

Bow

Chichen Itza

Chichen Itza, in Yucatán, Mexico, was an important Maya city from around 600 to 1200CE. The city's temple, today known as the Temple of Kukulkan, dominates Chichen Itza. The temple was dedicated to Kukulkan, the feathered-serpent god.

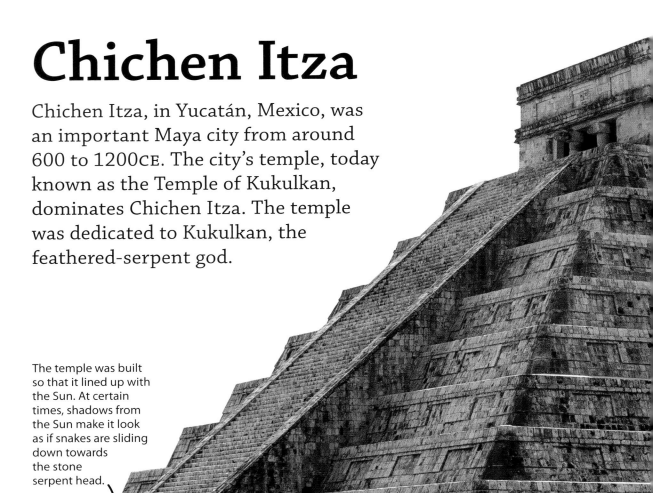

The temple was built so that it lined up with the Sun. At certain times, shadows from the Sun make it look as if snakes are sliding down towards the stone serpent head.

Sacred site

Chichen Itza was a busy trading city, but also a centre for religious rituals. Many of its most important sites were sacred places.

Sacred cenote

Sacred well
A cenote is a natural well full of water. Into it people threw gifts for the rain god. Gifts included gold, jade, pots, rubber, cloth, weapons, and even human victims. Some items were broken before being thrown in.

The temple has 91 steps on three sides and 92 steps on the fourth – 365 in all. This represents the 365 days in a Maya Sun year.

There are nine terraces leading up to the top. These nine terraces are split into two by a stairway on each side, representing the 18 months in a Maya calendar year.

Fifty-two panels are on each side of the pyramid. They represent the number of years in the Maya sacred cycle.

Stone temple
People probably gathered at the Temple of the Warriors for ceremonies. It had four stone platforms, and 200 stone columns on which were carved images of warriors.

Temple of the Warriors

Observatory
El Caracol ("The Snail") was an observatory used by Maya astronomers. Through carefully positioned slits in its walls, they checked the movements of the Moon, Sun, and stars.

El Caracol

Interview with...

Dr Diane Davies is a Maya history expert who has hunted for ancient objects and explored ruins deep in the jungles of Central America. She now lives in the UK, teaching schoolchildren and university students all about the Maya.

Q: Could you explain what an archeologist does?

A: Being an archeologist, I try to understand how people lived in the past by looking at the things they left behind – including their rubbish! Archeologists are like detectives that excavate (dig) for clues to find out what life might have been like in the ancient world.

Q: Why did you want to be an archeologist?

A: Growing up, I read a lot of adventure books and watched the *Indiana Jones* films, which inspired me to be an archeologist! I loved the idea of digging up the past and learning about how ancient people created amazing buildings without any modern technology.

Q: What's the most exciting thing about your job?

A: I find things that no-one else living today has seen before. Some artefacts are over 2,000 years old! As the first person to dig up and touch them, it feels like I am almost touching the past.

Q: Why did you want to study the Maya

A: I visited a Maya site in Mexico called Palenque while learning about Central American history. The rainforest, pyramids, writing, and art fascinated me, and I decide to learn more about these amazing people.

Q: What have you learnt about the Maya?

A: The Maya created one of the most advanced civilizations in the ancient world. They brought us extraordinary calendars, complex hieroglyphic (picture) writing,

Diane digging inside a Maya house

...nd some of the largest pyramids in
...he world. They also had a ball game like
...o other and, most importantly, chocolate!

Q: What's your favourite Maya fact?

A: The Maya knew all about the movements of
...he stars and planets. Venus was special to them,
...nd when they saw it in the sky they took it as a
...ign to go to war. This was called a "star war".

**Q: Where is the most exciting place
...ou have been for your work?**

A: I have worked in many places, from
...Vales to Peru, but the Maya rainforest in
...uatemala is the most exciting place for me.
...Valking to work with monkeys following
...ou from above is quite something!

Q: What's your most amazing find?

A: I helped to uncover the murals of San
...artolo. These are the earliest Maya paintings
...nd show how the Maya believed their world
...ame about. The murals date to around
...00BCE, over 2,000 years ago, and we found
...he earliest Maya writing from 300BCE. A
...elevision crew filmed us, and we appeared
...n newspapers because of the finds!

**Q: Apart from the writing at San Bartolo,
...hat's your oldest find?**

A: I found a beautiful red bowl in a Maya
...ouse. It was made around 100BCE and left
...ehind in 900CE! This meant that it was saved
...nd looked after for a very long time by its
...Maya owners.

**Q: Can you describe a typical day
...or an archeologist?**

A: In the Maya rainforest, I was often woken
...p by noisy monkeys. I spent the day with a
...eam of people digging in trenches to find

An ancient Maya bowl from one
of Diane's digs

pottery, stone tools, and even
human bones. After digging, I'd
sit down to examine the findings.

**Q: What sort of equipment do
you use?**

A: If I am excavating, I start with a
small pick to break up the soil. I then
dig with a trowel until I find something,
and use a small brush to gently get
rid of the mud.

**Q: Do you have any advice for
future archeologists?**

A: You have to work hard to be an
archeologist, but if you do well in
history and science in school then
you're on the right track to becoming
a history detective!

Art and technology

The Maya, Incas, and Aztecs did not use the wheel. Their tools were made of natural materials, such as stone. Yet they built boats and slung rope bridges across rivers. They made statues, huge temples, and beautiful objects. They studied the stars and maths.

Rope bridge

The Incas built rope bridges to cross wide rivers and deep gorges. They were used by messengers who could cover up to 240 km (150 miles) in a day.

Recording

The Incas kept careful records of everything, including llama herds, grain stores, and army numbers. Instead of writing, they used a system of knotted strings, called a *quipu*.

Stone carving

All three civilizations made detailed stone carvings, using stone tools. They created statues and carvings of gods. This carving shows an Aztec goddess.

click clack

Rubber

The Maya collected latex (sap) by "tapping", or cutting into, rubber trees. From it they made waterproof cloth, glue for books, and rubber balls.

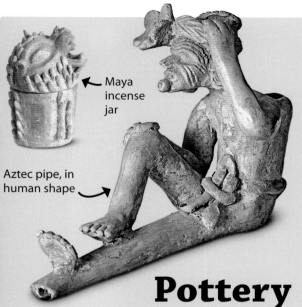

← Maya incense jar

Aztec pipe, in human shape →

Pottery

People used plain clay pots in the home. Decorated pottery was used in religious ceremonies at temples. Potters shaped clay by hand, then baked the pot to harden it.

PAINTING

All three civilizations used bright colours in textiles and in paintings. When Spanish soldiers arrived in Mexico, the Aztec emperor sent artists to paint them. This Maya wall painting shows warriors fighting during a battle.

Reed boat

The Incas paddled canoes made from reeds on Lake Titicaca, high in the Andes mountains. They went to sea on large rafts built from logs.

Music

The Aztecs made music for ceremonies, dancing, and in battle. They played a drum made from a hollowed out log, called a *teponaztli*.

Writing

The Maya created an early form of writing using signs, called glyphs. Some were picture-signs standing for ideas or words, others were sound-signs for parts of words. See if you can match the descriptions below with the symbols, and so decode the glyphs!

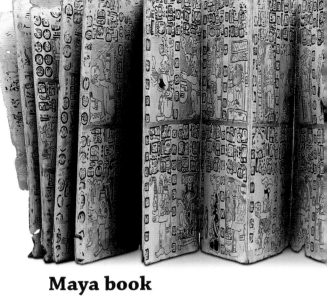

Maya book

The Maya wrote on paper made from bark. They folded pages to make a book called a codex.

"lady"

This is an easier one to start with! A woman's face, shown sideways.

"water"

Look for dots for raindrops. And can you see slashed lines for rain?

"Sun"

The Sun was important in Maya belief. Try looking for flower petals.

"to scatter"

Farmers scattered seed by hand – so look for the hand-sign.

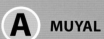 MUYAL

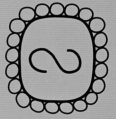

 K'AK'

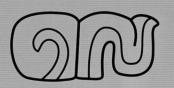

 IX

 WITZ

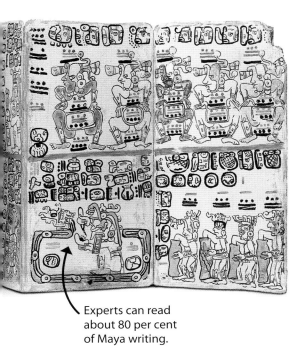

Experts can read about 80 per cent of Maya writing.

Maya numbers

The Maya counted in 20s. They used a dot for "1" and a bar for "5". They had a special sign for zero, or "0". The Maya were one of the first people to use the zero. Below are the Maya numbers 0–12, 15, and 20.

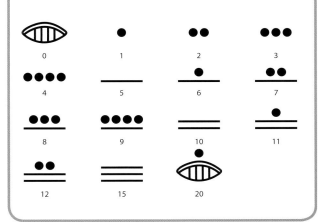

5

"fire"

Can you see the curved lines that look like flickering flames?

6

"cloud"

Can you spot the curved line surrounded by lots of small circles?

7

"mountain"

This is tricky! The glyph has three peaks, like a mountain.

8

"snake"

The feathered serpent was a Maya god. Can you see a serpent-head glyph?

E JA
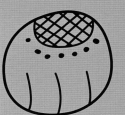

F CHAN

G CHOK

H K'IN
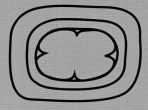

Medicine

If you were a Maya, Inca, or Aztec, you'd ask the gods for help to heal your illness. Plants were also important for healing the sick, and surgeons knew how to patch up battle wounds. These medical skills, however, could not fight off the killer diseases later brought by Spanish invaders.

Rabbit's foot fern
Aztecs used these leaves to make cough mixture and to treat arthritis (stiff joints).

Pudding pipe tree
Pods from this tree were eaten to help Mayas and Aztecs who couldn't poo.

Palm nuts
Oil and seeds from palm trees made skin, chest, and stomach medicines.

Surgical tools
Inca surgeons used sharp stone knives to carry out operations.

Trepanned hole in an Inca skull

Trepanning
Drilling a hole in the skull (trepanning) was thought to release evil spirits in unwell people.

Aztec doctors
This book, made by the Spanish invaders, shows Aztec doctors treating patients.

Peppers
Aztecs believed that eating peppers would stop them feeling sad.

Jade
People wore jade stones as charms to keep them healthy.

Snakeroot
These plants were used to cure snake bites and to help Aztecs sleep.

Cocoa beans
Aztecs used these to treat asthma, chest infections, and stomach upsets.

God health
Some gods were linked to special types of healing. Cihuacoatl was the Aztec goddess of childbirth. Women prayed to her for healthy children.

Cinchona bark
Incas made this tree bark into a medicine called quinine to treat a disease called malaria.

Mexican marigolds
These flowers are said to have been used by Aztec priests to make victims sleepy before human sacrifice.

Morning glory
An Aztec mixture made from this flower's seeds sent people into a trance-like state.

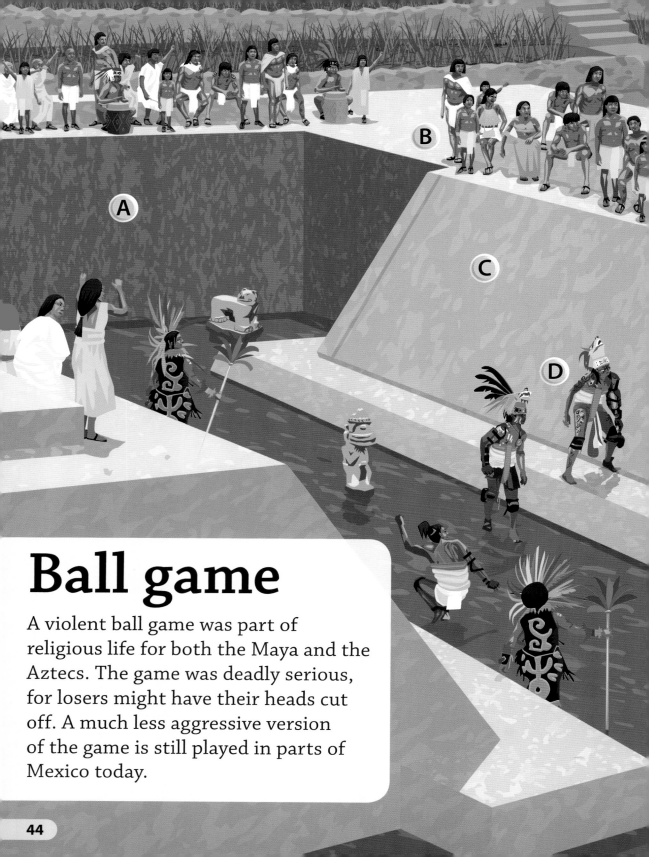

Ball game

A violent ball game was part of religious life for both the Maya and the Aztecs. The game was deadly serious, for losers might have their heads cut off. A much less aggressive version of the game is still played in parts of Mexico today.

WHAT'S WHAT

A **Court** The capital L-shaped court had sloped walls. Some were as long as a soccer pitch.

B **Spectators** People watched from platforms on either side. They cheered and shouted for their own team.

C **Sloped walls** Players ran up the steep side walls in their efforts to score.

D **Player's gear** Teams had two or three players. They wore headdresses, belts, and pads on their arms and knees.

E **Rubber ball** The heavy ball of latex (tree rubber) was hit with hips, elbows, or knees.

F **Stone rings** To score, a player hit the ball through one of two stone rings.

G **Scoring** The rings could be 6 m (18 ft) high, so it was difficult to score.

H **Captive players** Captive enemies always lost. Winners were given model heads (or real ones).

Calendars

The Maya and the Aztecs had several calendars. This meant that each day had more than one date! These calendars helped people to keep up with their busy schedules of religious celebrations.

Making a date

To see what the date was, a Maya combined a glyph showing the day name with a number between 1 and 13.

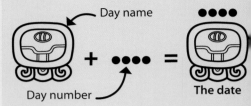

Day name

Day number

The date

Tzolk'in calendar

This religious Maya calendar had a year of 260 days. Each day had a date made up of one of 20 gods' names and a number between one and 13. Priests foretold events for different days.

A picture called a glyph was used to show the name of each day.

Maya numbers made of bars and dots gave each day a number up to 13.

! WOW!

The Maya believed that the world **started again** every **5,130 years**.

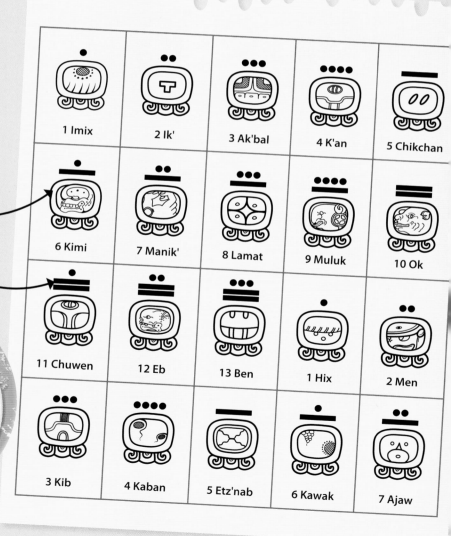

1 Imix	2 Ik'	3 Ak'bal	4 K'an	5 Chikchan
6 Kimi	7 Manik'	8 Lamat	9 Muluk	10 Ok
11 Chuwen	12 Eb	13 Ben	1 Hix	2 Men
3 Kib	4 Kaban	5 Etz'nab	6 Kawak	7 Ajaw

Haab calendar

Like our calendar, the Haab had 365 days. However, there were 19 months instead of 12. Most of these months had 20 days, with one month having five left-over days at the end. This was called the Wayeb.

Solar calendar

The Haab calendar was 365 days long because that is how long it takes the Earth to move around the Sun. This is called a solar calendar, because "solar" means related to the Sun.

Stone calendar wheel
The glyphs for the Haab month are carved around this wheel.

The 19 outer glyphs each show a month.

The Wayeb
The five Wayeb days were seen as unlucky.

Crafts

Children learned crafts from their parents. They could make pots and baskets, and weave wool and cloth. Craftwork was a full-time job for many people. Precious stone masks, metal jewellery, and feathered headdresses all took a lot of skill and practice to make.

Inca dish the shap of a turt

Pottery

People shaped wet, messy clay into pots and stamps by hand. Pots were coloured and decorated using powdered minerals. To make the clay objects harder, they were fired (baked).

Aztec stamp

Maya vase

Plugs were worn in holes in the ear lobes.

Maya earplugs, made from shell

Jewellery

Necklaces of precious stones and gold were made for nobles. The Incas liked turquoise (a blue-green stone). The Maya and Aztecs preferred green jade. Warriors wore gold plugs in their pierced ears and lips.

The gold plug was fixed into a person's lip.

Inca beads

Inca necklace

Aztec lip-decoration

Masks

Gold or precious stones were used to make masks. Mosaic masks were made from wood covered with pieces of stone. They were worn for ceremonies or to scare enemies in battle.

Inca gold mask

Maya mosaic mask

Threads were woven together into material.

Aztec loom

Inca woven textile

Weaving

Plant fibres and animal coats were spun into thread or wool. Aztec women wove cotton thread into light clothes, while Inca women made llama and alpaca wool into warm clothes.

Aztec fan

Feathers

Feathers were a sign of importance. They were used to decorate nobles' clothes, as well as shields and fans. Thousands of bird skins used for featherwork were found in one Inca city.

Inca pouch

Figure of a Maya woman weaving

Inca gold

Gold was the sacred metal of the Incas. They called gold "the sweat of the Sun god". But the Incas' fascination with gold led to their downfall. Spanish soldiers heard of a land of gold and silver, and conquered the Inca Empire so they could take their treasures.

Gifts of gold

The Inca emperor took gold and silver from peoples defeated in war. The emperor showed his power by filling storehouses with gold and by giving gifts. He also rewarded brave soldiers with gold.

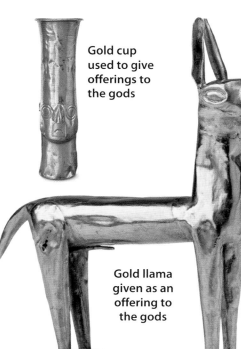

Gold cup used to give offerings to the gods

Gold figure of a god

Gold llama given as an offering to the gods

Gold of the gods

This magnificent gold disk shows the face of the Sun god, Inti. He was the Incas' supreme god.

This is a copy of one of the few precious Inca objects found that Spanish soldiers failed to melt down.

Golden nuggets

The Incas dug gold mines in the Andes mountains. Chunks of small gold rocks, or nuggets, were smelted (melted) until soft and then shaped.

The lure of gold

In the 1530s, Spanish conqueror Pizarro heard about the riches to be found in Peru. He and his men fought the Inca people, and stole and melted down most of the Inca gold. Only a few pieces are left in museums today.

Spanish gold coins

The Incas shaped gold into decorative ornaments, like this gold disc.

Under attack

In the 1500s CE, the Spanish came to the Americas to find treasure. They attacked the Maya, Aztecs, and Incas, whose lands were rich in gold and silver. The native people bravely fought back, but were conquered by the Spanish invaders.

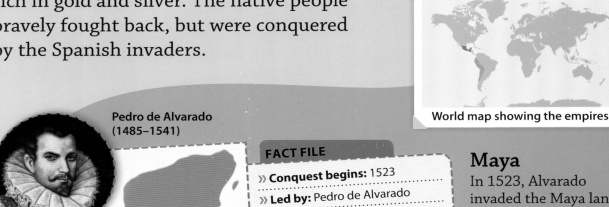

World map showing the empires

Pedro de Alvarado (1485–1541)

FACT FILE

» **Conquest begins:** 1523

» **Led by:** Pedro de Alvarado

» **Arrival site:** Soconusco

» **Major Spanish victories:**
Zapotitlan
Acajutla
Lake Atitlan
Quetzaltenango

Maya

In 1523, Alvarado invaded the Maya land One of the last Maya rulers, Tecun Uman, was killed during batt in 1524. Alvarado claimed to have won the land for Spain. The Maya fought on for many years.

Maya lands

Soconusco
1523   Quetzaltenango
             1524
Pacific   Zapotitlan
Ocean   1524
         Lake Atitlan
         1524   Acajutla
                     1524

Incas

Atahualpa had just won a war for the Inca leadership, but then Pizarro arrived with a small army and killed him. Another Inca leader, Manco Capac, fought back, but was killed in 1545. The last Inca leader was beheaded in 1572.

FACT FILE

» **Conquest begins:** 1531

» **Led by:** Francisco Pizarro

» **Arrival site:** Tumbes

» **Major Spanish victories :**
Cajamarca
Cusco
Vilcabamba

Pacif
Ocea

Aztecs

When Cortés invaded Aztec lands, the Aztec Emperor Moctezuma II sent gold to show his power. Cortés took the emperor prisoner and captured the capital city of Tenochtitlan.

Hernando Cortés (1485–1547)

Atlantic Ocean

Otumba 1520

Veracruz 1519

Tenochtitlan 1521

Cholula 1519

Aztec Empire

Pacific Ocean

FACT FILE

» **Conquest begins:** 1519

» **Led by:** Hernando Cortés

» **Arrival site:** Near modern-day Veracruz

» **Major Spanish victories:**
Cholula
Otumba
Tenochtitlan

Francisco Pizarro (1471–1541)

bes

Cajamarca 1532

Vilcabamba 1572

Cusco 1533

Inca Empire

How were they defeated?

The Spanish caused divisions within the Aztec and Inca Empires. They gained allies from these divisions and from local enemies. The Spanish had steel armour, swords, and guns. They also brought diseases, which killed many people.

Steel armour

Where are they now?

Today, many people in Central and South America have Maya, Aztec, or Inca ancestors. In Mexico, some people speak Nahuatl, which comes from the Aztec language. Other people in Central America speak types of Mayan. In Peru, many people still use versions of the Quechua language of the Incas.

Traditional Quechua dolls

Quechua
About 25 per cent of people in Peru speak the Inca language Quechua. Many Quechua people farm and make clothes from the wool of llamas and alpacas, following the traditions of their ancestors.

Top, or *huipil*

Nahua
The Nahua people of Mexico are descended from the Aztecs, and many speak Nahuatl. Some are farmers and craftspeople, like their Aztec ancestors. There are about 2.5 million Nahua people living in Mexico today.

Woven basket

Maya

The descendants of the Maya live mostly in Guatemala, Honduras, and Mexico. Many Maya live in small villages. Here they farm and carry on traditional Maya crafts, such as weaving. Others live in big cities.

Festivals

There are festivals celebrated throughout this region that combine old and new traditions with religious rites.

Dance of the Flyers
This five-man show is based on an Aztec rain ceremony. While one man stands on top of a pole playing music, the other four dangle from ropes, twirling to the ground.

Inca Sun Festival
Inti Raymi, the Sun Festival, takes place in many places in Peru on 24 June. It marks the shortest day of the year, and the start of the Inca new year.

Skull mask

Day of the Dead
This festival (31 October–2 November) mixes Christianity and ancient traditions. In Mexico, many people dress up and wear masks. They visit family graves with flowers and gifts.

Then and now

If you've ever bounced a rubber ball, crossed a suspension bridge, or eaten popcorn, you have the Maya, Incas, and Aztecs to thank! As well as being inventors, they were among the first people to discover many materials and popular foods of today.

Modern herbal medicines use passion flower.

Popcorn

Corn was first popped over fires in the Americas thousands of years ago. Later, Aztecs introduced it to the Spanish invaders, who showed it to the rest of the world.

Tortillas

Many people in the Americas made dried maize into flour. They baked maize flatbreads, or wraps, which the Spanish invaders called tortillas ("little cakes").

Maize tortillas

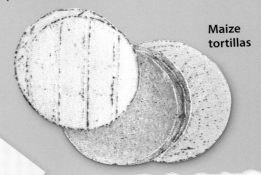

Chocolate

The Maya and Aztecs used cacao beans to make a hot drink, which they flavoured with chili. This spread to Europe, where it was called "drinking chocolate".

Cacao beans were called cocoa beans by the English.

Plant medicines

The Aztecs loved flowers and flower-medicines. They used passion flower to calm people, relax muscles, and help people sleep. This plant is still used in herbal medicine today.

A sapodilla tree

Chewing gum

The Maya found that sap, or "chicle", from the sapodilla tree went rubbery when chewed. Chewing gum was made from natural chicle until the 1940s.

Suspension bridges

The Incas built bridges to cross deep rivers to get to their mountain cities. They hung suspension bridges across the gaps using plant fibres. The bridges swung, but were safe!

Freeze-dried potatoes

Rubber

The Maya took sap from rubber trees. They turned the sap into squidgy, bouncy rubber by mixing it with juice from morning glory vines.

Rubber tree sap

Freeze-drying

The Incas left potatoes out to freeze during cold nights. They then trod on them to get rid of any moisture, drying them out. These freeze-dried potatoes, called chuño, lasted for a long time.

57

Facts and figures

There is so much to learn about the Maya, Incas, and Aztecs. We've gathered together as many fascinating facts as we could fit onto these pages.

The Maya didn't have sugar. They ate honey as a sweet treat.

8 MILLION PEOPLE SPEAK A VERSION OF THE INCA LANGUAGE, **QUECHUA,** TODAY.

The word **jerky** comes from the Inca word **ch'arki,** for dried Llama meat.

24,000

The Incas built roads stretching around 24,000 km (15,000 miles) across their vast empire.

6 MILLION

There are around 6 million Maya people alive today.

Maya children

The Maya pyramid the **Temple of the Jaguar,** at Tikal, rises **47 m (212 ft) high.**

This is equivalent to around **10 giraffes** stacked on top of each other.

Aztec children

may have been pricked with **maguey cactus spines** as a punishment.

THE MAYA KEPT A LOOK OUT FOR

VENUS

AND MAY EVEN HAVE STARTED WARS WHEN THEY SAW IT IN THE MORNING SKY.

90%

Up to 90 per cent of the Aztecs and the Maya died when the Spanish came, mostly from European diseases.

700

It is said that 700 sheets of gold were used for the walls of the Inca Golden Temple in Cusco, Peru.

650

In 2017, archaeologists digging beneath Mexico City found 650 skulls of human sacrifice victims.

Glossary

Some words in this book may be new to you. This is what they mean. They will help you to learn about the Maya, Incas, and Aztecs.

alpaca Animal of South America and a relative of the llama and camel, valued for its wool and hunted for meat by the Incas

Andes Highest range of mountains in South America, which stretches along the western side of the continent

armour Body protection for soldiers

astronomy Study of the Sun, Moon, planets, and stars

calendar Chart showing a year or years divided into units of time, such as days

canal Waterway made for boats, or to bring water to crops growing in farmers' fields

canoe Small boat made from a tree trunk or animal skins, and pushed through the water with paddles

Central America The strip of land joining North America and South America

ceremony Special event that is often religious

chinampas Small islands in lakes, used by the Aztecs as farmland to grow food

civilization Large group of people, or society, who share the same way of life

codex Book with handwritten pages

conqueror Winning side in a war, when one leader defeats another and takes their land

empire Multiple lands ruled by one leader

glyph Picture signs, used by the Maya and Aztecs in writing instead of alphabet letters

irrigation Bringing water from rivers or lakes to farmland by digging canals

llama The Incas' most useful domestic animal, providing wool, milk, meat, and transport

maize Commonly known as corn, or sweetcorn, an important food in the ancient Americas

Mesoamerica Earlier name for the area of land that includes Central America and Mexico

mummy Dead body preserved by chemicals or drying so that it does not decay

noble Important person in society, often a royal relative who may control an area of land and people

obsidian Hard, volcanic rock used to make sharp-edged knives and war weapons

priest Person who leads religious ceremonies

pyramid Stone-built mound with four triangular faces and steps, often with a temple on top

...uipu Knotted-string device
...sed by the Incas to record
...vents, keep accounts, and
...nd messages

...tual Religious activity in
...hich people perform a series
... set actions

...cred Linked to the gods

...crifice Offering, such as
...ld, food, or human victims,
...ade to the gods to seek
...eir help

...te A piece of ground used
...r something, such as an
...d city

...ave Person owned by other
...ople, and made to work for
...em without pay

...ciety Group of people living
...gether in an ordered way, for
...ample in a country

...mple Building for religious
...remonies and worship
... gods

...rraced fields Walled fields,
...ch as steps or terraces one
...ove the other, created by the
...cas on mountainsides

...rrior Soldier who is trained
... fight in battles

How to say it

This guide will show you how
to say words and names from
the Maya, Inca, and Aztec
civilizations. Capital letters
mean you should emphasize
that part of the word, or say
it a tiny bit louder.

Feather shield

Acajutla (A-ka-HOOT-la)

Acatitlan (A-ka-TEET-lan)

atlatl (at-LAT-l)

Cajamarca (Ka-ha-MAR-ka)

cenote (sen-oat-ay)

Chichen Itza (Chi-chen It-za)

Cholula (Cho-LOO-la)

Choquequirao
(Cho-keh-KEY-ra-o)

chuno (choo-no)

Cihuacoatl (Si-WA-ko-at-l)

Cinteotl (Sin-tay-ot-l)

curacas (koo-RA-kas]

Cusco (Kus-ko)

huaca (hwa-ka)

Huayna Picchu
(Hway-na Pee-choo)

huipil (wi-pill)

Huitzilopochtli
(Hwit-zi-low-POK-tli)

Illapu (Il-A-poo)

Intihuatana (In-tee-WA-ta-na)

Ixchel (Eesh-chel)

Machu Picchu
(Ma-choo Pee-choo)

Mama Coya (Ma-ma Koy-a)

mamakuna (ma-ma-KOO-na)

Mama Quilla (Ma-ma Key-a)

maquahuitl (ma-KWA-weet-l)

Maya (MY-a)

Otumba (O-TOOM-ba)

panacas (pan-A-kas)

Quetzalcoatl
(Kwet-zal-ko-ATL)

Quetxaltenango
(Kwet-zal-te-NAN-go)

quipu (key-poo)

Sacsayhuaman
(Sak-say-WA-man)

Sapa Inca (Sa-pa In-ka)

Tenochtitlan (Te-nock-TEET-lan)

Teotihuacan (Tay-oh-ti-WA-kan)

Tlaloc (Tla-lok)

Tonatiuh (Ton-a-TEE-ooh)

tzolk'in (zol-keen)

Vilcabamba (Vil-ka-BAM-ba)

Viracocha (Vir-a-coach-a)

Willac Umu (Wil-ak Oo-moo)

Xipe Totec (Shi-pay toe-tek)

Zapotitlan (Za-po-TEET-lan)

Index

Acknowledgements

Dorling Kindersley would like to thank the following people for their assistance in the preparation of this book: Polly Goodman for proofreading, Helen Peters for the index, Dan Crisp for illustrations, Mohammad Hassan for map illustrations, and James Tye for additional photography. The publishers would also like to thank Dr Diane Davies, Maya Archeologist, www.mayaarchaeologist.co.uk, for her interview on pages 36 and 37.

The publisher would like to thank the following for their kind permission to reproduce their photographs:

(Key: a-above; b-below/bottom; c-centre; f-far; l-left; r-right; t-top)

1 Alamy Stock Photo: Eduardo Mariano Rivero 2 Dorling Kindersley: Richard Leeney / Whipsnade Zoo (crb). 3 Dorling Kindersley: Tim Parmenter / The Trustees of the British Museum (bc). Dreamstime.com: Max Ddos (br). 4 Alamy Stock Photo: Lucas Vallecillos (bc). 5 Alamy Stock Photo: PRISMA ARCHIVO (cra). Dorling Kindersley: Tim Parmenter / The Trustees of the British Museum (bc) 6 Alamy Stock Photo: PRAWNS (br). 7 Alamy Stock Photo: Granger Historical Picture Archive (bl). 8 Getty Images: De Agostini / G. Dagli Orti (br). 9 Getty Images: De Agostini / G. Dagli Orti (bl). 10 Alamy Stock Photo: Paul Fearn (br). 11 Getty Images: DEA PICTURE LIBRARY (bl). 13 Alamy Stock Photo: ART Collection (cra). 14 123RF.com: Luca Mason (tl). Alamy Stock Photo: Jiri Vondrous (tr). 15 Alamy Stock Photo: The Granger Collection (tl). Getty Images: DEA PICTURE LIBRARY (tr).16 Alamy Stock Photo: Peter Horree (clb).18 123RF.com: Eric Isselee / isselee (br); Абаджева Марина (c/Opossum). Dreamstime.com: Monypat7 (cra); Leon Rafael (tr). Getty Images: Andia (cl).19 123RF.com: Warut Chinsai / joey333 (br/honeycomb); martinak (cb/ mushrooms). Alamy Stock Photo: Stockbyte (clb/ squash). Dreamstime.com: Felinda (cl/Papaya); Robert Red / Red2000 (cra/beans). 20 Alamy Stock Photo: ART Collection (c). Dreamstime.com: Leon Rafael (c). 21 Alamy Stock Photo: J Marshall - Tribaleye Images br. Dorling Kindersley: Andy Crawford / Pitt Rivers Museum, University of Oxford (tr); Richard Leeney / Whipsnade Zoo (c). Getty Images: Science & Society Picture Library (tc). iStockphoto.com: Mark Kostich (c). Rex Shutterstock: Granger (c). 24-25 iStockphoto. com: mariusz_prusaczyk. 24 Alamy Stock Photo: Granger Historical Picture Archive (cl). 30 Alamy Stock Photo: Granger Historical Picture Archive (c); Heritage Image Partnership Ltd (tr). Getty Images: Print Collector (bc). 31 Alamy Stock Photo: Granger Historical Picture Archive (tl); Eduardo Mariano Rivero (tl); Heritage Image Partnership Ltd (cr). 32 Alamy Stock Photo: Tom Grundy (ca). Dorling Kindersley: Andy Crawford / National Museums of Scotland (clb); Michel Zabe / CONACULTA-INAH-MEX (cra, c, bc, b). 33 Alamy Stock Photo: Heritage Image Partnership Ltd (tc); INTERFOTO (crb); Mostardi Photography (bl). Dorling Kindersley: Michel Zabé (tl); Andy Crawford / University Museum of Archaeology and Anthropology, Cambridge (c);

Michel Zabe / CONACULTA-INAH-MEX (bl/Stone axe, br); Dave King / Museum of London (br/arrow). Dreamstime.com: Carl Keyes / Ckeyes888 (cr). 36 Dr. Diane Davies: (tr, br). 37 Dr. Diane Davies: (tr). 38 123RF.com: Kriangkrai Wangjai (br). Alamy Stock Photo: imageBROKER (cl). Dorling Kindersley: CONACULTA-INAH-MEX (bc). iStockphoto.com: andyKRAKOVSKI (c). 39 Alamy Stock Photo: Heritage Image Partnership Ltd (bl); Emily Riddell (br). Dorling Kindersley: Gary Ombler / University of Pennsylvania Museum of Archaeology and Anthropology (tc, tl). Getty Images: DEA / G. DAGLI ORTI (cr). 40-41 Dorling Kindersley: Michel Zabe / CONACULTA-INAH-MEX (tc). 42 Alamy Stock Photo: blickwinkel (tr); Speshilov Sergey (fbl); North Wind Picture Archives (bc); Phanie (cr). Dorling Kindersley: Michel Zabe / CONACULTA-INAH-MEX (cl, bl). Dreamstime.com: Edwardgerges (br). 43 Alamy Stock Photo: Manfred Ruckszio (bl); Valery Voennyy (tc). Dorling Kindersley: Michel Zabe / CONACULTA-INAH-MEX (tr, c). Dreamstime.com: Matthias Ziegler / Paulmz (ca). Getty Images: Universal History Archive (br). 47 Alamy Stock Photo: Sabena Jane Blackbird (b). Dorling Kindersley: Jamie Marshall (tr). 48 Alamy Stock Photo: Heritage Image Partnership Lt (cl). Dorling Kindersley: Michel Zabé (br); Gary Ombler / University of Pennsylvania Museum of Archaeology and Anthropology (tr, c); Andy Crawford / National Museums of Scotland (cr, bc. 49 123RF.com: ylstock (tl). Alamy Stock Photo: Giulio Ercolani (tr); Mostardi Photography (bl). Dorling Kindersley: Andy Crawford / National Museums of Scotland (cr); Michel Zabe / CONACULTA-INAH-MEX (c, br); Andy Crawford / Pitt Rivers Museum, University of Oxford (bc). 50-51 Alamy Stock Photo: Deco (c). 50 Dorling Kindersley: Angela Coppola / University of Pennsylvania Museum of Archaeology and Anthropology (cl); Andy Crawford / The Trustees of the British Museum (c); Tim Parmenter / The Trustees of the British Museum (bc). 51 Dorling Kindersley: Chas Howson / The Trustees of the British Museum (br). Dreamstime.com: Joools (tc). 52 Getty Images: DEA PICTURE LIBRARY (cl). 53 Alamy Stock Photo: Heritage Image Partnership Ltd (cla, cb). 54 Alamy Stock Photo: John Mitchell (cl). Dreamstime.com: Max Ddos (tr). Getty Images: Robert Van Der Hilst (bc). 54-55 Getty Images: Hugh Sitton (bc). 55 123RF.com: Kairi Aun (tr). Alamy Stock Photo: M. Timothy O'Keefe (c). Dreamstime.com: Barna Tanko (tl). 56 Getty Images: Frederic Cirou,PhotoAlto Agency / Isabelle Rozenbaum (bc). 57 123RF.com: drpnncpp (bc); Nutthawit Wiangya (tr); Sven Schermer (crb). Alamy Stock Photo: imageBROKER (cl). 58 Dreamstime. com: Alle (tc); Daniel Wiedemann (cl). 58-59 123RF. com: Ulf Hbner (c). 59 123RF.com: Vitaliy Markov

(bc); Zhang Yongxin (ca). NASA: JPL (cr). 61 Alamy Stock Photo: INTERFOTO (tr). 62 Dorling Kindersley: Tim Parmenter / The Trustees of the British Museum (tl). 64 123RF.com: ylstock (tl).

Endpaper images:
Front: 123RF.com: Matyas Rehak (Tikal); Alamy Stock Photo: Art Collection 2 (Manco Capac), Granger Historical Picture Archive (Alvarado), Sabena Jane Blackbird (Calendars), Roy LANGSTAFF (Roy LANGSTAFF), PRISMA ARCHIVO (Pizarro), Science History Images (Moctezuma II); Dorling Kindersley: Gary Ombler / University of Pennsylvania Museum Archaeology and Anthropology (Olmecs), (Aztec empire); Dreamstime.com: Sorin Colac (Chichen Itza); Getty Images: De Agostini / G. Dagli Orti (Yupanqui). Back: 123RF.com: Rafal Cichawa (Choquequirao), jejim (Inscriptions), Luca Mason / Ikpro (Kukulcan), Jason Maehl (Winay Wayna); Alamy Stock Photo: Paul Christian Gordon (El Tepozteco) Heritage Image Partnership Ltd (Santa Cecilia, Acatitlan), Kuttig - Travel - 2 (Ollantaytambo); Dorling Kindersley: Linda Whitwam CONACULTA-INAH-Mex (Pyramid of, the Magician); Getty Images: Jason's Travel Photography / Flickr (Jaguar); iStockphoto. com: stockcam (Templo Mayor);

Cover images: Front: Alamy Stock Photo: J Marsh - Tribaleye Images br, Eduardo Mariano Rivero l; Dorling Kindersley: Andy Crawford / Pitt Rivers Museum, University of Oxford cr, Chas Howson The Trustees of the British Museum cr/ (doubloons), Gary Ombler / University of Pennsylvania Museum of Archaeology and Anthropology tr; Dreamstime. com: Barna Tanko cb/ (basket); Rex Shutterstock: Granger c; SuperStock: Prisma / Album alb1469844 cra; Back: 123RF.com: Sven Schermer cla, ylstock r; Dorling Kindersley: Gary Ombler / University of Pennsylvania Museum of Archaeology and Anthropology cr; Spine: Dorling Kindersley: Gary Ombler / University of Pennsylvania Museum of Archaeology and Anthropology b; Front Flap: 123RF. com: Ulf Hbner (pyramid), Eric Isselee / isselee (lar Alamy Stock Photo: Giulio Ercolani (mask), Science History Images (illustration); Dorling Kindersley: Andy Crawford / Pitt Rivers Museum, University of Oxford (pouch), Dave King / Museum of London (arrow), Gary Ombler / University of Pennsylvania Museum of Archaeology and Anthropology (plate Dreamstime.com: Max Ddos (doll), Edwardgerge (papyrus), Matthias Ziegler / Paulmz (beans), Leon Rafael (stone); iStockphoto.com: andyKRAKOVSKI (kipu); Back Flap: 123RF.com: Audrius Merfeldas te iStockphoto.com: naumoid tr.

All other images © Dorling Kindersley.
For further information see: www.dkimages

My Findout facts:

Acatitlan
Mexico, Aztec
Early Aztec buildings in town of Santa Cecilia, Mexico State.

Templo Mayor
Tenochtitlan, Aztec
Snake head from huge pyramid-shaped temple in Mexico City.

El Tepozteco
Mexico, Aztec
Small temple made of two rooms. Dedicated to the god, Tepoztecatl.

Temple of the Great Jaguar
Tikal (Mutul), Maya
Made so that priests' voices carried to the crowds below.

Choquequirao
Peru, Inca
Imperial mountain stronghold-city, with 180 terraces.

Sacsayhuaman
Cuzco, Inca
Stone fortress at the Inca capital. It has walls about 18 m (59 ft) high.

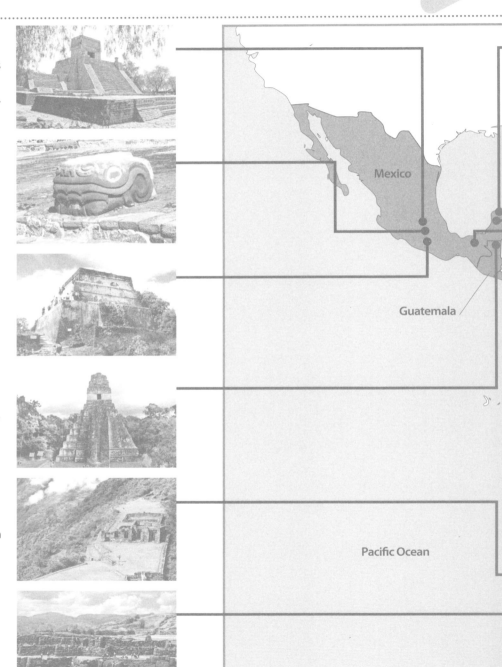

Mexico

Guatemala

Pacific Ocean